My Bucket List

Deborah Anne Tanzer

My Bucket List
Sand Sprinkled Poetry

Artworks by Barry W. Tanzer

Townsville's Fig Tree

My Bucket List: Sand Sprinkled Poetry
ISBN 978 1 76109 511 5
Copyright © text Deborah Anne Tanzer 2023
Cover image: *In My Lifetime*, by the author

First published 2023 by
Ginninderra Press
PO Box 3461 Port Adelaide 5015
www.ginninderrapress.com.au

Contents

In My Lifetime	9
The Awakening of the Rainforest	10
Climbing Mountains	12
Listen said the Old Man	14
How Love is Like Chimes!	17
Ode for My Sons	19
Christmas Lights	22
Spray of the Night Ocean	25
Esther's Shack	26
A Cold Winter's Night	29
How I Love Them	30
I am!	32
When We Were But Young	34
Agnes: the Queen of the Street!	36
How Great Thou Art – Just in This Moment!	39
Beacon to the Shore	41
Sparkling Fairy Sneezes!	43
The Stock Inspector	46
Lord, Give Him Strength	49
The Rising of the Sun	51
(Thank Our) 'Southern Lucky Stars'	53

In my lifetime,
I think that I may have walked upon a million grains of sand!
But Mum –
(…) that's a mere bucket full (?)

To the Lighthouse! – commissioned work for Barry's son Mathew Tanzer (Brisbane), oils

The standard is to write so that it spills forth, encaptivating one's disposition on Earth. More than words, consisting of heart, soul, and an abundance of love. In doing so, may they feel such pain or still their breath; till tears dwell or a smile spreads and touches hearts…thus leaving one's literary footprint on a soul, like footprints in the white sand.

Deborah Anne Tanzer, 2020

Barry William Tanzer, working on art titled *Tower Bridge*, acrylic and texture paste on stretched canvas

Beached!, acrylic on stretched canvas, Ross Creek, Yeppoon

In My Lifetime

I think
That I may have walked a million grains of sand
At times
The sand burnt me
At times
The water cooled my feet

For every shell I met
I made a friend and I met countless
Only few were special enough to remain in my thoughts
Those that washed out to sea
Were never meant to be

In my lifetime, I viewed a million sunsets
At times I sheltered my eyes from God's wonder
Frightened by its perfection
Other times I allowed his beauty to engulf my senses
Carrying me along with the rhythm of the waves

In my lifetime
I think
I was indeed fortunate
To have walked upon a million grains of sand

The Awakening of the Rainforest

(For my Mt St Bernard Boarding School Sisters, memories of the cold rainforest tablelands of Herberton, 1980–83)

Early morn chills my skin
A touch of fresh scarlet.
Mist settles in
Silently fogging my vision.

The native bird shrieks out,
Its glorious vocals rudely intrusive.
Hear the teasing and trickling of a nearby stream,
As it playfully jostles between trembling rocks and boulders

Dew freezes in juxtaposition,
Boasting sculptured teardrops on edges of leaves.
Burly branches stem majestically,
Discord amongst the down's softness.

Indigo, scarlets and ravishing golds,
Smudge the scenic canvas.
Chartreuse rudely interrupts and defiantly spits
On the tranquil harmony of flora.

Experience the vaporisation of the haze,
As filtered beams of sunlight cautiously invade
Aromas of shrill freshness
Subtly fill my head space.
Respectfully, time chooses to stand still in the warmth,
As peaceful serenity surrenders to its beams

Stealing my breath,
Young girls, children…
Captured by the awakening of the rainforest!

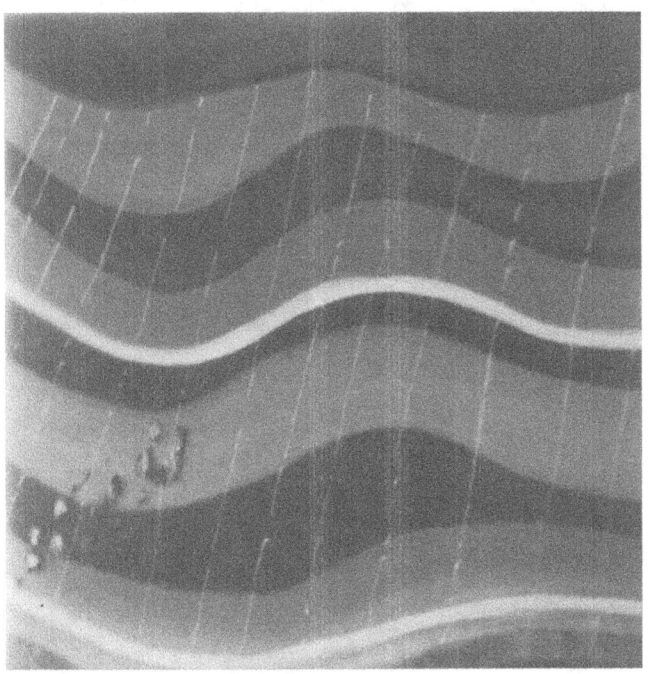

Coastal Showers, first attempt at an abstract, although some may see impressionism, She Speaks Gallery, Townsville, sold to *House Rules* (television programme)

Climbing Mountains

Take her as you see her
She needs to feel calm right now
Find a better way of living life
Speak little of such sadness
Talk only of joy dear friend

For she is feeling scared of things unknown
As her thoughts turn around
She is unsure of where she is
Find time to hold her
Reassure her
Caress her with gentle words of hope

Be kind to her please cause its hard you know
She is not to blame not this time
Strength must come of this
So she takes it slow
She needs only wade through the pain
Todays sorrow shall stay right now
To teach her strength and humbleness

But give her the time she needs
And you will see
She shall climb mountains in her life

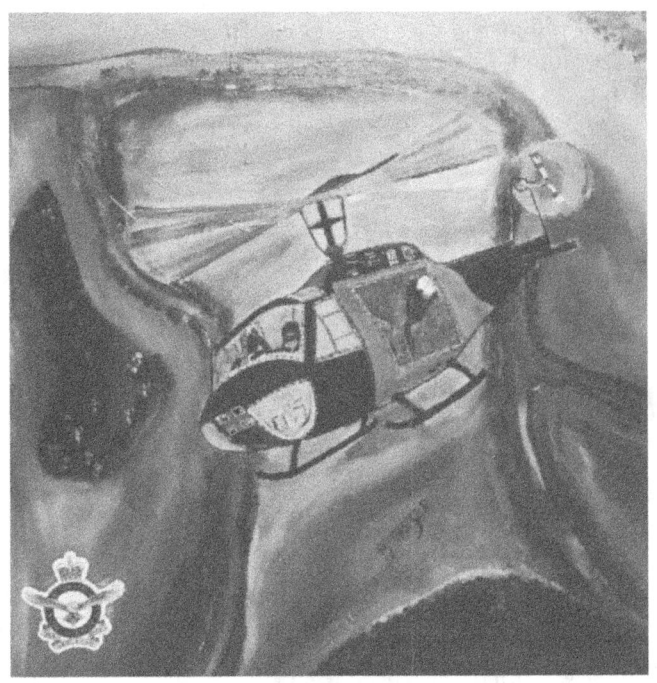

Vietnam

Listen said the Old Man

Listen said the old man
'Watch out for the wind
It brings a peace
Tenderness
Tranquillity
As it brushes one's face'

'Let us talk of the moon'
Watch their faces
Watch them let lose a smile
His eyes twinkle, not sad
'Walk in the rain
See how you laugh
Open your mouth
Taste the drops'

Sit in the sun with him
Feel how your body slumps
In the warmth of the tangerine rays
Relax in its touch

'Have you noticed the colours
In the leaves
On the trees?
Next time look
There are at least a hundred per leaf'
He assures us

'Apricot splotches
Reds of all shades
Browns crispy on edges
Sunburnt oranges'

Ile Des Pins – Danseur de Wapan
(painted after a trip to the Isle of Pines, New Caledonia)

Just take the time
To see in your darkness
And feel your breath
Disappear slowly

'I am
More than aged
I feel hurt and cry
I laugh and still wish to sing
I have a wealth of memories
In fact, I am no different from you'

'So take it all in
Like I do now
It will be over in a blink
So, blink as slow as you must.'

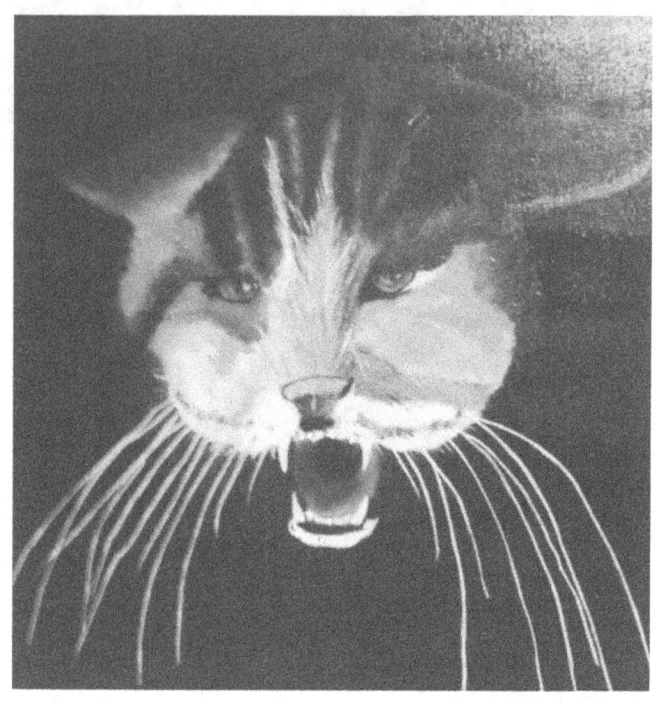
Out of the Darkness, a gift for the hospital PTSD coordinator

How Love is Like Chimes!

(For Les and Kerrilee; Mathew and Rio)

Stillness envelopes the moment
That love first saw one another
A tiny breeze shuffles at the stilled chimes
Creating a melodic clunk of flirtatious flutters amidst shyness

As the wind finds heart
Thus a song finds creation
Imitating precious moments
Where love's bond is primal and moulded

Crazed by the relentless winds now swarming in
The chime swings and crashes
CLANG!
BANG!
SWOOSH!
JINGLES!
Carried away on their own journey
Oblivious

Nothing stands in their way
Passion and desire
Replicating both sweet, sweet harmony
Yet strength in its delivery

Then sudden stillness falls again
Its silence deafening
Unpredictable
Quiet
Disturbing and uncomfortable
Replicating a true rollercoaster of relationship

Never consistently melodic
Strikingly beautiful
Yes, its momentum spirals
Depicting the dramatic human nature
That is love itself
Chimes of love
That inevitably sings a song of love always

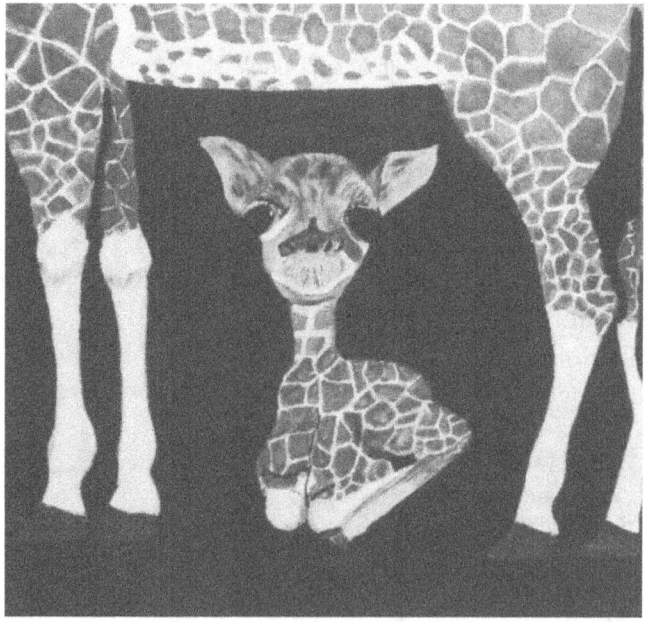

Out of Africa

Ode for My Sons

(My three musketeers, Cain, Gabriel and Samuel: with love always)

May the road you choose to take
Be the easier one
If it rains on your travels
May you collect the drops on your tongue

Be there rocks and boulders in your way
Lean on one another, always
Support your brothers and take it calmly in your stride
Prize the meek of doings
And acknowledge the efforts of the attempt

Turn your cheek to that which tempts
Resist change to that which already shines
If loneliness comes your way
Turn it to 'simply alone' for a time

The road is not laid with concrete
It is up to you to pave destiny
Perfection is not perfect, it breaks people
Learn happiness from mistakes

Individuality is a blessing
Sameness is a bore
Always choose to be the bigger man
Hold your brothers when you can
Apologies go a long way, so far

Nothing is more valuable than your love for one another
A brother is like your shadow
Laugh with one another
Cry when it is needed
Be silent in support and walk together always as one

The Cabinet Meeting, acrylic (synthetic polymer) and texture paste on stretched canvas, depicting parliamentarians Bishop (taller), Shorten and Rudd), commissioned for A Townsville Man Cave

Once you were but babes in my arms
I held you to my chest and protected you instinctively
I guided you the best I knew
I made mistakes, but never was it from lack of love
Fierce love and eternal

Remember – please remember
You are special
Believe and trust in that which you are

'You Are All That'
And so much more
You are my sons!

The Veteran, acrylic and texture medium on stretched canvas. Reminds me of a warrior/veteran. Do Elephants get PTSD? I think so, and that would account for the rogue ones.

Christmas Lights

(For Mother – Carol Ann – who has loved Christmas since…forever!)

See the colourful magical lights for Saint Nick, hear our
   kinfolk frolicking'
Christmas trees alit and décor's with bells
All in honour of Thy Lord up above

Little eyes all a twinkle, waiting eagerly
Count down the days till we see the Jolly Fat Man
Our fences all lit up with solar Chrissy' lights
Our windows all whitened with a pressured snow can

No pine trees, just store-bought ones
No snow, just stinkin' hot sun!
We somehow make the most of it all
Christmas tinsel, belly laughter and fun!

We read them stories of Christmas tales
Then the boys snore snug in their beds
The little tykes so hyped-up
With Santa dreams running round in their heads

I told them of a Santa who squeezes in through the whirly bird
On the tin roof
I tell them when they listen, deer hooves lift aloof
A list for Santa is posted with a special 'Mary' stamp
Signed carefully by the boys
Requesting computers instead of trucks and soldier toys?

Steaming Down the Murray, painted entirely with a palette knife using acrylics and texture paste, for Barry's grandsons, Cain, Gabriel and Samuel (my sons)

On Christmas morn they all arise so early
The look on their faces quite priceless
Ripping paper wildly off all their gifts
Who's cleaning up? Hmmm…one guess!

Christmas lunch gathered at Nanny and Pops
Hot roasts, steamed pudding and ice cream
Heavy, bloated and floating in the pool
As we listen to the kids play and scream

All the string lights around the world dance and sing
Blinking colours of red and green for Santa's surprise
Yet no light can compare, beauty or magical
As the light of joy remembered, in our children's eyes!

Three Old Boilers, acrylic and texture paste on stretched canvas, artist's wife (author's mother) Carol and her sisters, Cherie and Chelle, commissioned for Cherie

Spray of the Night Ocean

(For my brother Gene, who is 'the little boy fishing from the moon')

I am surrounded by glistening white spray…
Moonbeams magically dancing upon the darkness,
Waltzing to the rhythm of the oceans' melodic sonata
Blue violet tints the seductive waves…
Placing tinges of blood blue hues upon the horizon,
Entrapment of shimmers, cut sharply through the perfection
   of this canvas before me
Enchantment is complete

My gaze is hazed by the majestic awe that engulfs my vision
My senses take in the salty sting of the water's essence
I am silent, my limbs heavy
I am of totality, yet irrelevant
I am overwhelmed, but still…
The moon laughs at me…smirking with confidence
The conductor of this idyllic rhythmic concerto
Pulsing and unstoppable

I allow the ocean to nip at my ankles, with anticipation
Feeling the touch of its icy bite upon my warm skin…
It retreats with fulfilment, aware of my inapt presence
Magic moon sprinkle a little of your dust over me…
Allow your ocean to chime out its melody…
Ocean spray cleanses my fears,
Bringing clarity to my existence
We love you, Gene,
Always in our hearts…

Esther's Shack

Hidden among the shadowing trees
Autumn leaves reflecting the brown hues of the earth beneath
The darkened clouds above, hover longingly
Scents of fresh rain tickle through the atmosphere
Between the dense forest of tress and its leafy bushes
Look carefully
In the distance

A little shack made of wood and tin
Uneven beams held together
With timeworn nails and rusty wire
Its aged tin shutters held over its windows
By shattered old pieces of timber
Smoke rises steadily from Esther's chimney

The Strand's Jetty, Townsville, author's favourite piece

Wondering stranger, amongst the pine forests' bitter cold and
    frosty chilled air
Feel drawn to this little shack's warmth and homeliness
The old wooden door hinges are slow to open
The warmth of the fireplace hits you immediately
Followed by the lingering scent of tea leaves
Escaping from the tin billy on the vintage wooden stove

Old Esther motions with her frail hand for you to sit
As she shuffles around
You take in your surroundings
Lace curtains yellowed with time
Floral vases sit pretty on a nearby duchess
An oval mirror reflects a timber bed
Surrounding the bed is a patchy mosquito net

Townsville's Harvey's Range Roadhouse, commissioned and
displayed on the Harvey's Heritage Tea House wall

A teacup is placed in front of you
By a shaky pale hand
You gratefully place your lips on the rim of the cup
Ahhhhhh…
You soak in the bitterness of the brew
Relishing in the aromas rising from the cup

She silently watches you
Taking in your movements
Time has stood still
in Esther's shack.

Pioneer Cottages

A Cold Winter's Night

As I sat by the fire
On a cold winter's night
I thought 'how lucky'
That we have the fire's light!

… Because we would freeze,
While the snow dropped a shape so nice,
And even the fowl's water
Would turn to ice.

No, I don't really like winter,
No, not at all..
But I like the way
The snowflakes fall!

Written by a very young Deborah aged seven in the 1970s, in a little country town called Injune, Queensland, Australia. Written in class, praised by a teacher – in her praise, she created a love for writing poetry. To praising children for those little achievements.

How I Love Them

(For George & Patricia, Leslie & Betty – grandparents like no other)

How I love them, so very much
Time has moved on (how quickly it seems)
Bring them back to my memories – into my heart dear Lord

I sense her smile, the slight tilt of her head, laughter from her mouth
Smells of lavender and roses waft through my nostrils
Her dressing table array with jewellery and lipsticks
I watch her dress and choose her shoes, her dresses are many

Mesmerised by her movements
I am captured now by her presence as I sit on her bed

My vision of maturity and loving arms
I watch her sit on her bed to put on her chosen shoes
All the while she is chatting to us about life
Her past, filling our cups of knowledge, memories of her
    childhood
Her legacy

Pioneer Cottage

Red Cedar Logs, depicting Clydesdale draft horses pulling logs

In another room, listening to his races on a small transistor radio
He smells of man cologne and sweat from a hot day
His clothes ironed and neat
Lines around his mouth appear in that smirk
I see him reach out his hands, a working man's hands
I picture a younger me, as I climb onto his lap
He looks kindly, lovingly into my eyes

I rest my head on his chest and fall asleep
She kisses him on the head as she walks by (in those chosen shoes)

How I miss them, but smile at the memory
I can hear them say 'this too shall pass girly – and we shall meet again'

I am!

I have learnt to live life in the moment
Tis of no opportunity nor is it of any meaningful purpose
For one to dwell on the past

Look forward in anticipation
Exceed self-limits and set up for inevitable falls
To live in this moment seems just and fair

Indeed, any other way would seem almost self indulgent
Who are we to be worthy of more
We are honourable in meekness
A simple race, complexity bought about by language and emotions

I am but a breathing mass of thoughts, beliefs and values
Little more than a flashing thought in the entirety of God's plan
I shall exist

So shall I continue to breathe
So shall I stay 'in this moment' and k.i.s.s.
Keep It Simple Soldier!
I have learnt not to expect more than that next step
Foot in front of foot…in front of…in front of…

Each moment of pain reminds one that we merely exist
Each moment to rekindle the notion that we are privileged
Don't waste time on negatives or mistakes
Nor is there wish to expel them from the core, they are the
  learning of all

I listen
I look
I speak if need be

I see my hands aloft
In front of my eyes
Therefore I know that…I exist
Therefore I know that…I am!

One Tree Hotel, acrylic on stretched canvas. Once a staging post for Cobb & Co., made famous by Banjo Paterson's 'Hay and Hell and Booligal'. Commissioned by sister, Ann Marie, Ipswich.

When We Were But Young

(For my brothers, my…everything: Les, Mathew and Gene)

When we saw through the eyes of a child
A butterfly flutters by – or is it a flutter by?
Whatever…indeed worthy of a chase!

The lights of the Show, enthralled and captivated our little minds
The taste of fairy floss on a stick
Was it floss or melting magic of a strawberry cloud?

Soft grass and down underneath our legs
Linking chains of flower daisy's
To present a lemon pearl neckless to the Princess (*me)
Running and jumping through a long-grassed sweet meadow
Our feet lifted just a little and we took weightless flight

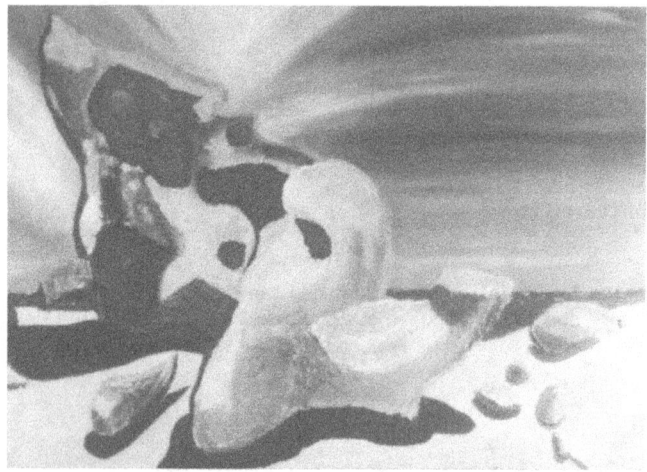

Remarkable Rocks, inspired by the artist's visit to the great landmark on Kangaroo Island and kept by the family

Tinkles and darling (missed) little Gizmo!, artist's son Les (and author's brother) adored family pups

Cascading locks of bouncing bobble hair
Embracing our round faces, framed us like lions
Almighty fierce – little cubs
Youth took us on its inevitable journey through the maze of imagination
Sadly, a journey that fades as these years take hold

Sit down, take a load off
Think back to our younger years
Through the eyes of a child
Every sibling fun memory is still there, waiting for you to unlock it
Give it due credit and think back
Feel the breeze wrap around you in that meadow of our laughter
Engaged in that memory – and we shall never forget our bonds, through being young.

Agnes: the Queen of the Street!

How do you feel old Agnes?
How has the sand timer treated you, lovingly, gently?

I see you Mall Shuffle with your shopping trolley and assorted bags
It would seem, that time has not been kind
And those nearby smile and whisper at your presence

You don't take notice, nor care, nor mind
Lines haggardly etched through your once glorious face
Your thin arched fingers still famously display your rings
A collection of cloudy glass emeralds and plastic pearls
Your frail cracked lips wear your scarlet seductive shade of 'rose stick'
You smile, thinking that those around are bowing from the hip and applauding you
In your mind, that is what the whispers are about

Your floral dress raggedy and dirty, floats gently around your waist
Your skinny frame, bones rattling like teeth knocking
Cigarette smoke curls magically and wildly up around your face
Your telltale face, kisses at your royal aura and you are proud of your trolley

Clutching your glittery rhinestone handbag, complete with missing clasp
Your eyeliner is smudged, heavy eyelids have shadowed your once almond eyes
Through a squint of rolled skin
Eye slits of elephant wrinkles
They twinkle still and defiantly look down on your subjects
Still whispering behind your back

Awkward Elegance

You move with tiny grace
Each step effortless, with a hobble that is timely

Shuffle your frail little frame
Swing your precious bag, jingling saved pennies
JINGLE
SWING
JANGLE
SWASH

Oh we notice you dear Agnes!
We are taking you in, on our zealous watch
With fascination…

You feel!
You ARE worthy, unique, individual and special!
You the once stunning beauty, rare and shining
A treasured jewel adored by men through the ages
Reeking of class and style, not the stench of old rags and dirty streets
Your Queen Status still becomes you Agnus..
'Work it Girlfriend'…
…and don't let the Bastards get the best of you!

Edna (Hello, possums)

How Great Thou Art – Just in This Moment!

I gaze upon thine endless beauty
A radius of pinks and oranges roll out in front of my eyes,
Like waves frolicking on a tide
Horizons rolling with glorious mountains peaks and
    concaving diving valleys
The wonder of the scale, the greatness, engulfs and
    encompasses our wholeness as a planet

Standing still – frozen in time
Standing still – shallow in breath
Standing still – quiet grace, resolve and wonderment

Stun us and grace us with your beauty
Your innocence is lost among your bounding strengths
Your ancient timelessness
History marks on nearby boulders and tree trunks

Take it all in wise child
Take it all upon your shoulders, relish and harness this
Its energy, its gifts…in this moment in time
It is now yours to protect and grow with
For all of us to keep and cherish
Respect this land and it will teach us graciousness
Teach us to live in the now

The responsibility will flow over into a calm for one another
Breathing in the chilling swirling droplets of air from her tears
Be here as one, with Mother Earth, nowhere else – in the now!

Parrots, silk painting, commissioned by dearly loved sister (in-law) Chelle, Townsville

Beacon to the Shore

Co-written with musicians Les and Cain

(Verse)

When I'm aching and I feel so insecure
Feels like I'm shaking
Love comes to get me

My bodies aching
and I feel so insecure
Just can't make it through the pain

(Chorus)

Two hearts as one
Two dreams become
As you walk in through the door

Reflections, city fireworks, Brisbane

Just look my way
And soon you will see
You'll be my guiding beacon to the shore

(Verse)

When I'm hurting just can't cut through the pain
Feel so deserted
I can't take this again
Somebody, take me
To the shore

Sparkling Fairy Sneezes!

(For my nephews, nieces, aunties, uncles, cousins...for all the joy and the memories!)

I am not perfect...
Just a sweet sneezy funny girl
My crepe paper wings still a little crooked and ripply
I fluster over heavy brown leather clogs
As they are dragging down my flying launch

My tousled hair brown like toast
Wild and wispy, like my unicorn's tail
My dress a mere crumpled old paper bag
As my pet mouse is wearing my good dress (sigh)

Little more than a tinkerbell of sorts,
Yet wise mermaid's knowledge of the old
I know that if you believe in me...
Then I am indeed enough!

With your love, my wings start to flutter and spread
Tossing out fairy dust, across the room it sprays
It starts up sneezing as it floats through the air glistening
Powdery fairy dust messing up Mother's blue carpet
Only with your love though,
Can trust rise and my star will start to shine

And only then...will I raise my arms
And sprinkle golden particles of rain
Tis your belief and encouragement alone,
That can make me smile
Bringing forth cherry blossoms from the corners of my smile
Watch me as

I SPARKLE
I DANCE
I SOAR
I AM…enough – I am 'Glitter, Imagination, lined with Honey'
Bundled in a bubble of hope and never-ending love!

Don't Fence Me In, acrylic on stretched canvas. Artist's sisters, Diane, Lynette AnnMarie and Marilyn all have commissioned works. This is one, purchased by Marilyn Tanzer, Ipswich.

Grand Old Lady, black and white charcoal and pencil,
commissioned by artist's sister Diane Clark, Toowoomba

The Stock Inspector

(For my father, Barry William, stock inspector, who taught us love for the bush, to handle dust from the cattle and to enjoy Slim Dusty's music)

Cold crisp dew lingers gently upon his face
First sun rays
Sneak through the limbs of the old blue gums
Smells of the dirt mingled with fresh eucalyptus leaves
Waft up through the foggy morn
Wake up
Wake up
Echoed whispers from the bush

He hears the cattle stirring nearby
Their noise makes him feel a sense of belonging to the earth
Familiar and comforting

Resting Horse Teams, on Harvey's Range, Townsville pioneer days

Riding Shotgun, acrylic on stretched canvas. Barry's own personal experiences as a stock inspector involved in the eradication of TB and brucellosis in Queensland.

The crackle of the firewood as the billy starts to boil
A black cockatoo flutters from branch to branch
Intrusively interrupting his morning awakening

Wipes the sleep from his eyes
He arises from the warmth of his canvas swag
As the freshness of the cold air bites at his arms
It jolts him into sudden awareness

The stillness of the barren dry land is almost deafening
He looks around and silence governs him
A nearby creek lies lifeless and empty
Leaving nothing and promising little
A nesting kookaburra shrills its disappointment

He quietly takes in his old mate, under his tattered and dusty Akubra
A silent nod takes in his presence as he hands him a steamy tin cup
Unspoken respect between the old ringer and his mate
They will ride long today, many hours of tough saddle ahead
Very little will be said
Kerchiefs blocking the dust of the cattle dancing
Movement will be slow and measured up and down the parched gullies

Water will be scarce among these red relentless basalt plains
Time drags on but this is all he has ever known, his heart lives for this land
The stocky longs for the sun to go down
As he whoops at the cattle to 'move it on up'

Lord, give him strength

(For all those lost in grief)

Your piercing howls
It breaks through the shameless night
Finally, your quivering body resolves into a slump
You tug your hoodie over your sodden head
Little comfort from the pelting squall
It's time to find another alley
To sleep away so tired so weary
Fallen sparrow without its nest
Alone
Forgotten
Time seems lost
Hunger growls deep and dark within

Deer in the head lights
Run run run
Little fawn
Rain splashes tenderly down
Unsympathetic, a puddle mocks at your feet
Stand still, stagnant, catch your breath

Feel raindrops from heaven
Fall on your mouth – Gasp
The flood gates open and your tears spill
No need to hold back
Vulnerable exposed, screamer of the night
A moment in time
For you are now– feeling like the homeless man… Lord, give him strength

A Tragic Loss. RIP Harambe, Silverback shot in the USA after a child fell into the enclosure. While not commenting on his destruction, I can express my feelings that he should not have been there in the first place.

The Rising of the Sun

As the sun sets in defeat, I listen for the sizzle and steam off the ocean's horizon
The chilled night air stings at my skin
Nostrils gently fill with the smoke from the campfire

Beneath my toes those 'million' sand grains scratch at my skin gently
I am reminded by the silence; the deafening silence…
That for all our hustle and bustle of life's journeys
In the end we are alone, within our own minds' thoughts

Anxiety, sadness, poverty, loneliness…
Anger, fears, traumas…all seem non-existent
In the finality that is 'the end'

All that matters, is the contentment in your soul
The gratification in your heart
As it expands and swells with the love you have known
The treasured memories you have left behind
The proud legacy you have delicately crafted

No matter how exhausting and hard the road winds
No matter how hot the sun burns on your face
No matter how strong the winds push against your back
Know that the sun will honourably set one day, in the very end.
Yet, there will be a sunrise again the next day for those we leave lovingly behind
Reminding them to constantly look for the love and joy in the morning sunrise,
Always a constant reminder of my adoration for them
Beyond the melting sun and tranquil horizon.

Hope – Trust – Faith
Live life to its edge…
Until we see one another again in God's Heavens

(Thank Our) 'Southern Lucky Stars'

We seek knowledge of how to truly exist,
Spinning in this carousel world...
Blurred spaces collide in real time,
Grasping at breathtaking moments...
Evolution divine.

Our Nation is rich with political freedoms
Like a molten gold chalice...
We drink from its cup,
Engaging, and learning...
A thirst-quenching sup.

While neighbouring Countries scream out in the dark,
Tired, persecuted and lost...
Human resilience ultimately gives,
Enduring senseless wars...
Where genocide furtively, pointlessly...lives.

There are millions that go hungry, lands stricken with drought.
Fevered jungles, dense highlands
Where babies die off each day,
While we, 'The Privileged Country'
Capitalists, whining about pay.

Embrace this 'lucky' country, dip your toes in its sand.
Beneath diamond skies and sapphire oceans,
Hazy reflections, aloft Southernly Lights.
A land rich in ethnicity, engorged with diverse culture...
Unapologetic progress, attest to human rights.

.

Rainforest canopies umbrella, endangered native fauna.
Majestic ferns, mangroves, streams, offer shielding habitat.
Wet tropics meet scattered reef, priceless beauties beyond measures.
Dolphins leap through sunset horizons, near Migaloo whale…
Oceans rhythmic and alive, with immeasurable natural treasures.

Travel this world, absorbed, in all its glorious splendour!
Boat the Nile, climb pyramids, view Africa's ravenous beasts.
Niagara's spray will chill as it strikes upon your face,
But for the most memorable of visits…
This land, 'Australia'…takes first place!

As a lucky country, a land safe, loved and treasured.
Though best etch in our memories, thus we may never forget…
We are still part of a global network, a scattering of place,
A brotherhood of collective nations,
A Unity – Forever, One Human Race!

www.ingramcontent.com/pod-product-compliance
Lightning Source LLC
Chambersburg PA
CBHW071037080526
44587CB00015B/2658